PASSION
— TO —
PROFIT

ANIK SINGAL

THE 7 SIMPLE STEPS TO TURNING YOUR PASSION INTO REWARDING PROFIT

START YOUR OWN ONLINE BUSINESS TODAY

PASSION TO PROFIT
Copyright @2016 by Anik Singal

Lurn, Inc.
12410 Milestone Center Drive, Suite 600,
Germantown, MD 20876
Second Edition
www.lurn.com
ISBN-13: 978-0-9972079-8-9

ARE YOU READY TO TAKE THE FIRST STEPS TOWARD YOUR GREATEST POSSIBLE LIFE?

Thirteen years ago, I was right where you are now.

I was hungry. I was determined. I was ready to make a change.

But I didn't only want to take control of my life. I wanted to make a name for myself. I wanted to make a difference in the lives of thousands of people.

My dream seemed unreachable. I had $100, no experience, and no technical knowledge.

I had no idea what I was doing. I had no formula, no system... and no direction.

But I knew one thing: I had to release the inner entrepreneur that was busting to get out.

So what did I do? I spent 14 hours every day scouring the Internet and asking everyone I knew for one breakthrough idea.

Once in a while I'd get a glimpse of hope, even if it was false. I fell victim to many misleading online ads and get-rich-quick schemes.

I tried idea after idea, and I continuously failed.

It went on for months. 18 months, to be exact.

Even though it was painfully clear that I knew nothing about making money online or starting my own business, I kept trying. More than anything, I wanted to take control of my life.

I wanted to do something big, leave a legacy, and live my life my way!

i

It was a pretty big task, but my dreams finally came true.

Not from luck. Not from coincidence.

It took relentless dedication and bold perseverance.

I finally discovered the no-fail, step by step system to success.

Fourteen years later, I helped contribute to over $100 million worth of digital products sales - in particular, information products.

If you told me 14 years ago that I was going to build a $10 million a year business around something as simple as digital information, I would have laughed. Then I would have asked you sincerely, "What the heck is digital information?"

When I started out, I had no idea about online business. Back then I was actually trying to find a franchise or a store to buy. Which is pretty funny seeing as I had no money.

After weeks of searching random keywords on Google, I finally landed on something called "Internet Marketing."

I did not believe that I could make money from home, right on my computer.

Internet marketing seemed too good to be true. I almost dismissed it – except I happened to come upon an incredible Internet forum. I started reading discussions between real people who were making hundreds of thousands of dollars.

These people were just like you and me - except they were making tons of money from home, on the Internet, right from their computers.

And how were these people making that kind of money?

Simple. They were marketing information online.

I knew immediately that I had just discovered THE hidden goldmine.

I had found the answer!

My life was about to become sunshine and lollipops! I fantasized about the millions I was about to make.

But there was a problem.

I beat my head against the wall for a long time. I couldn't find anyone to guide me; to show me the direction I should take.

It took over 18 months to make my first dollar online.

Why?

Because I was working with no system and no steps. I was discovering the process on my own. It was a major struggle, and it was going to get a lot worse before it got better.

It was 548 days - 18 months - before I made any money. One. Measly. Dollar.

But that hard-fought dollar changed my life.

It can change yours, too. It won't take nearly as long, though, because my decade of pain is now your greatest asset.

I have tried - and tracked - literally every strategy that's possible in this business model. After years of trial and error, building and teaching this system, I have now created the easiest way to start your own online business.

Here's how you do it:

1. Aggregate information into a simple online course, using a step by step formula.

2. Publish your information online, where you keep all the rights and you also get 100% of the profits.

3. Follow a simple marketing model to start generating sales, revenue, and income.

There you have it. I call this process "Digital Publishing."

Digital publishing is largely responsible for the **$100 million** in products I've helped sell online (including my own products, affiliate products, and client products).

Digital publishing is why I've been privileged to teach over 250,000 students worldwide.

Digital publishing is now a **multi-billion** dollar industry.

Digital publishing has helped me become one of this generation's leading online marketers. It's why I've been privileged to win awards from *Businessweek, Inc. Magazine, Inc. 500*, and countless others.

Just look around. Digital publishing is now the way almost everyone reads, learns, and grows.

Make no mistake: Digital publishing can be your ticket to starting and growing the business (and the life) of your dreams, because:

1. You'll be immersed in your passion. You get to spend every single day doing what you love.

2. With your own profitable business, you'll enjoy incredible freedom. You'll be your own boss, work when you want, and spend more time with your family.

3. There's no glass ceiling on your income or your business growth. Grow as big as you want!

Unlike 14 years ago when I started, today you have the greatest opportunity. Everything you need to know is instantly available – and I'm about to hand it to you right here, right now.

In the following pages, I'll share how you can build that lucrative business and fulfill your dreams.

Being extraordinary begins right now.

Anik Singal
CEO & Founder, Lurn, Inc.

TABLE OF CONTENTS

INTRODUCTION

WHY THE WORLD NEEDS THIS BOOK

The world needs this book because you are special. I'm not flattering you. You are truly special because you are unique. You have a wealth of knowledge that's uniquely yours.

You have unique experiences and skills that people all over the world want to learn. Maybe your special knowledge is your passion. Maybe it's a hobby.

Maybe it's something that you're an expert in because you've been doing it for years. It could be anything. A craft, a sport, a better way to do something.

You might be thinking, "But I don't have a passion, a hobby, or expertise."

That's impossible.

Everyone on earth has knowledge and expertise that can truly help thousands of others. But even if this is a concern of yours, keep reading. I promise you'll walk away with your eyes opened - and a business you love.

My goal is to teach you a life-changing business model, open your eyes, and show you an amazing opportunity to work with me and my expert team!

This is really important for you - and for others. Digital publishing (or "information marketing") goes far beyond just earning a fantastic income for yourself. Your special knowledge will help countless others. Maybe even hundreds of thousands of lives.

This is your chance to leave behind a true legacy. This is your chance to change your life, change the world, and build a solid future of financial freedom.

And if I can do it, so can you. I don't have a doctorate in business. I've never been an executive in a big company. I inherited no family bloodline for business.

But what I have is even more valuable: **Passion.**

I love all things related to entrepreneurship. I live it. I breathe it. My brain never turns off. I look at a new business like an artist looks at a blank canvas. It's a true passion. It might even be an obsession.

I live the life of an entrepreneur. I have thousands of hours of sweat equity. In that time, I've accrued an enormous wealth of knowledge. I honestly believe this education goes miles past even a Harvard degree. I have "on the job" training that I've been forced to learn through mistakes!

I will help you avoid all of those very same mistakes.

I'm now blessed to have helped thousands of students start their own businesses and take full control of their lives.

The best part? It's easier, faster, and more effective to build your own digital publishing business than it has ever been before. Seriously.

You could not have chosen a better time to start your information business than now. Digital Publishing is the #1 booming industry in the world - and you're at the cutting-edge of it all right now.

So why aren't more people doing it?

The answer is simple. Most people have no idea this business model even exists. I actually got some shocking results recently when I conducted my own survey among published authors.

I asked them the following question: "Do you know that you can easily make a full-time income by simply marketing your information online, and that you can earn anywhere from $100,000 to millions?"

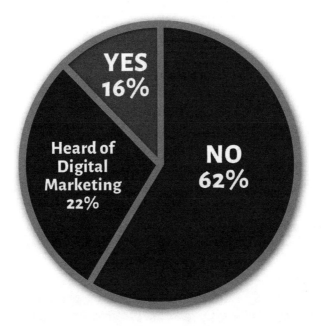

62% of everyone I asked answered, "No." Can you believe that?

Even among those who are in the content business, over 62% of them have no knowledge of this business model! Only 16% said they knew they could earn six figures or more - and I can tell you that most of them aren't taking advantage of that fact.

Digital publishing generates billions of dollars in sales every year. And it is about to hit its greatest growth spurt right now.

This is it.

You have found the #1 way to build the life of your dreams.

MY TRUE MISSION

My mission is to create over 1000 digital publishers. These 1,000 people will be able to take full control over their financial futures while serving the world to make it a better place. The question is if you want to be one of the 1,000 people?

All you need is a true passion to create excellence, to change your life, and to help others around the world with your knowledge.

If you're ready to get started, I'm ready to share my entire story with you. I'm going to give you every step you need to start your business.

You can do all of this yourself, and I'm here to help you through the process.

But before we start, we must agree on one thing...

I believe in digital publishing. I have seen many of my students make a great deal of money with it, but it is **not** a path to instant wealth.

This is not a get rich quick plan. There IS no such thing.

I'm not telling you this for legal reasons, or because I'm required to by the FTC. I'm not even telling you this because it's the right thing to do.

I'm telling you this because it's important to me that you and I are on the same page.

You see, like anything else in the world that can change your life, you have to dedicate time and hard work to succeed. You have to apply yourself. Realistically, it's going to take a little time. You have to do this right, and you have to make sure that the business you create is top notch and adds real value to the online community.

I can show you tons of examples. I can tell you hundreds of stories. I can even show you dozens of income proofs. And I will. But these are all about people who take action.

The case studies in this book are about people who really implement what they learn. They don't stop at small obstacles. Like everyone else, they have good days and they have bad days.

There are no guarantees. There never are.
Just remember that you have me and my entire team here to support and

work right alongside you. As long as you follow the steps in this system, there's nothing that can stop you.

Commit yourself to learning and taking serious action. Do that and you'll put yourself in the best possible position to enjoy a rewarding business for life.

Now get ready to take action.

CASE STUDY: DAWN CLARK
THE DIFFERENCE IS IN THE SYSTEM [1]

As a single mom with three kids, Dawn Clark's life used to be way out of balance. In order to make the income necessary to support her family, she would spend all of her time working. Her goals were to spend more time with her children, less time working, and to have more money to pay the bills.

I wish I could say I introduced her to digital publishing. That's not true. As an accomplished expert in the personal development space, Dawn had been creating digital products for almost 9 years.

Through digital publishing, she was able to find the freedom and income she wanted. Rather than building a life around her business she was finally able to build a business around her life. She even put her three kids through Ivy League schools!

But she wanted more. More opportunities and freedom. She started engaging with us. She followed my proven system for creating and marketing a digital publishing product, and her business grew between 400% and 500%.

For nine years, Dawn created and marketed a quality digital product. But as soon as she found my system, her sales skyrocketed!

---

[1] These results may not be typical nor expected for every person. This is not a "get rich quick" scheme. Your level of success in attaining similar results is dependent upon a number of factors that are not the responsibility of Lurn, Inc. These factors include your skills, ability to follow through, dedication, network, and financial situation, etc.

CHAPTER 1: MY ACCIDENTAL JOURNEY

HOW A $100 BILL GREW INTO A $100 MILLION BUSINESS MODEL

When I share my journey with people, their eyes widen. Their jaws drop.

Not because I'm some super human genius who holds the world's only predictable path to online success. But because the steps I've used in my journey can easily be copied, pasted, and duplicated by anyone.

In fact, they have been. Thousands of times.

This is why I'm sharing this with you today. I know you can take what I teach you and start your own incredible journey.

I know that deep down, you know it, too.

$100 IN MY POCKET

I remember it like it was yesterday. The only money I had to my name was $100.

I was studying hard in college with the hope that I would graduate and get a nice, comfortable job. The plan was to work hard and grow. One day, I would make enough money for a comfortable life.

The problem was that I hated that plan. It was not enough. Not for me. I wanted more. Much more.

I've had an entrepreneurial spark since I was a child. I've always had the passion to chart my own destiny.

Even at a very young age, one of my favorite phrases used to be "I'm my own boss."

But I didn't only want great wealth. I wanted to be an entrepreneur, because I knew that it was the best way to do something good for people. I knew that being an entrepreneur was the only way to make a truly positive difference in the world.

The problems were my fear and my lack of knowledge. I didn't have anyone to guide or mentor me in starting a business and becoming my own boss. So I went to college to become a doctor. It seemed to be the next-best profession to pursue.

My education in medicine was short-lived.

Within a few months, I knew I wasn't going to make it. Medical school just wasn't going to cut it for me. So I went out looking for a solution.

My childhood fantasies of being an entrepreneur came back and I turned to the only "friend" who I thought could help: Google.com.

I typed the words "how to make money" into the search bar. I went through every type of business opportunity that you can imagine, from stuffing envelopes to filling out surveys. They all seemed like scams to me.

Then I learned about franchising. "That's it!" I thought. With franchising, I could just take someone else's system and duplicate it. It was perfect!

There was just one little problem...

	Minimum Cost	Maximum Cost
Franchise Fee	$20,000	$20,000
Initial Ad Fund Contribution	$5,000	$5,000
Leasehold Improvements & Site Fees*	$59,150	$121,400
Additional Funds for 12 Months	$12,000	$45,000
Grand Opening Advertising	$10,000	$12,000
Training, Travel, & Living Expenses (per participant)	$1,500	$2,500
Insurance	$1,500	$2,400
TOTAL	$109,150	$208,300

No matter how much research I did, the results were the same. I needed at least $100,000 to properly start my own franchise.

That wasn't all. I also needed to devote myself full time to the endeavor. Considering I was a college student with a very aggressive class schedule, that just wasn't going to happen.

Disappointed but still detrmined I kept my search going. I could feel in my heart that there was an answer for me somewhere out there. I just had to find it.

After months of repeatedly seeing the phrase "make money online," I decided to do a Google search. Little did I know that that would be the day my life changed.

With a search term like "make money online," you can imagine how many illegitimate offers I had to read through and ultimately push aside.

One day, after months of scams, I came upon a website that changed my life: An Internet forum.

This forum was full of regular, everyday people who were claiming to make tens of thousands of dollars per month online.

The amazing thing was that they were real people - entrepreneurs who I could message, and even talk to! For the first time in my life, I felt I had found a legitimate opportunity, and real people who could actually help me!

I started asking tons of questions. Practically every answer came back with very similar advice: Find something you're good at, put up an information product about it, and count your millions.

Perfect! I knew just what to do. Ever since I was a child, I had always aced school. I always got the best grades.

I was never the smartest kid in class. I just had really effective studying strategies. I could cram for the hardest exam the night before and break the curve – scoring the best in the class. (Of course, 24 hours after the exam I forgot everything I had memorized.)

I was well known in college for my strategies. My friends knew, my family knew... even my college professors knew I had some kind of system.

As a matter of fact, my friends and other students started fighting just to study with me before exams. My professors even started having me give lectures to their classes on how to prepare for an exam!

I loved doing it. I felt I was helping everyone. I would constantly get praise for it.

So when I needed something to sell on the Internet, I had it! There are millions of college kids. These kids spend thousands on their education. More than 50% of these kids never get through college.

The best part? There was not a single program like this on the Internet.

Wow! I was a genius! I figured I would be a millionaire overnight. I just had to create my own "How to Study in College" program and throw it on the Internet.

I would run some ads, sit back, and watch my millions pour in.

As you probably already guessed, things didn't go exactly the way I had planned. I wish I had the system that I'm about to give you now. I would have saved myself a lot of misery and pain.

Instead, I spent 7 long months on this product. I worked day and night. I skipped classes. I skipped my friends' parties. I never went to a single basketball or football game. I became a robot in my room working on the best product of my life.

After all, this was going to make me into an overnight millionaire, right?

Well, launch day finally came. I ran back from class to my dorm room computer. I hit the "LIVE" button and sat down, staring at the screen.

For hours... and hours... and nothing happened.

Days went by and I didn't have even a single sale.

I was heartbroken.

Worse, I was now in debt. I had spent my $100, and I had even used my father's credit card. I was $300 in the red.

I remember staring at the computer that day in near panic. My dreams had come crashing down. Had I been lied to this whole time? Had I just wasted all that time? Was it all just a colossal sham?
No.

I wasn't going to give up just yet. I realized that I may have temporarily failed, but there had to be a great lesson in all of this. I realized that my "earning" for now was in my learning.

I sat down and wrote out what I had learned:

1. Don't be over-confident, and don't go it alone. Follow a proven step-by-step system. It's safer, quicker, and better than trying to figure it out on your own.

2. Don't be the first person in a niche. The fact that no one else is doing it is a BAD thing, not a good thing. Competition is good.

3. Get help. Get coaching. Ask someone for guidance. Drop your ego and your skepticism.

The bottom line was that in that temporary failure, I learned one of my greatest lessons, the one that has helped me make millions since then: Start with a complete step-by-step system.

HOW ONE NIGHT'S SLEEP BEAT 18 MONTHS OF WORK

Ultimately, my entrepreneurial spirit prevailed. For the next 9 months, I tried just about every way under the sun to make money online. I was determined to find the right system. With every mistake I made, I learned new lessons.

I tried every business model under the sun:

- eBay
- Affiliate marketing
- Writing content and making money from ads
- Pay per click ads
- Blogging

No matter what I tried, it didn't work. I never stopped. I kept at it.

But every man has a breaking point, and I was reaching mine fast.

The problem was that no digital marketing "systems" existed back then. There were only a handful of people making money online - and most of them would never reveal what they were doing.

After failing for months – it had been 18 months since I had started – I had had enough. I remember it like it was yesterday. I had had another exhausting day of trying to make money online. Another day of failing.

I caught my reflection in the mirror and practically screamed. "What are you doing? You've done this for 18 months and have nothing to show for it!"

I gave myself one final ultimatum: 24 hours. That was it. If I didn't make a single dollar online in the next 24 hours, I would end my entrepreneurial dream. I would go back to doing what everyone else was doing. I would go get a job.

I knew that giving myself this final 24 hours deadline meant I had to give it everything I had. I stayed up late, banging away at my keyboard.

This night was different, and I was hopeful. I felt like something was going to happen.

Why? Because for the first time in 18 months, someone had reached out to me and actually gave me a plan. That person gave me a step-by-step system and even showed me an example.

This was my last chance. Everything was riding on it. I did just as he said. I worked until 3 in the morning. My head was literally falling on the desk before I finally finished.

The next morning, I sprang out of bed. My heart was pounding. I was beyond nervous. I raced over to my computer, tripping over my shoes and almost hitting my head on the desk.

I logged into my account...and there it was staring back at me.

My account showed that I'd made $300 overnight! I had made more money in 6 hours sleeping than I had made in the past 18 months combined. I couldn't believe it. I rubbed my eyes and refreshed the page again. There it was!

I had finally made money online.

I can't even tell you how it felt. It was absolutely the best feeling in my life.

What did I do differently that time, after so many different ways to make money online? What was it that finally worked? **It was the system!**

I had followed a friend's proven system, step-by-step. Not 30% or 50% of the system. 100%. The whole enchilada. And it worked like magic.

Following this system, I learned a lot more than how to make $300. I discovered how to repeat that result again, and again, and again.

Over the next 60 days, I repeated the steps in the system many times and was able to make my first $10,000.

HOW I DISCOVERED THE SCALABLE DIGITAL PUBLISHING BUSINESS MODEL

All this time, I was merely promoting a one-page review website. I had simply written a one page ugly website review of a particular software that I had mastered.

In my review, I had linked to the software's own sales page using my "affiliate link." This means that every time someone clicked from my review page to the software and bought it, I earned a 50% commission!

All I had to do to keep these sales going was use a few traffic building secrets.

That only took me about 1-2 hours a day. Of course, I was incredibly excited to report my newfound success to my friends over at the forum. After all, these were the people who had been answering my questions for well over a year now.

Something very interesting happened as soon as I put up my story on the forum. The forum members saw that I was an expert at the software that I had reviewed.

Within one day, I got a very intriguing private message: "I'll give you $500 if you can install this software on my own website."

It used to only take me 3 hours to install this software on a website - which was fast in those days. This meant that I would be paid over $150 an hour for work that was nearly mindless! Feeling blessed, I accepted his offer and he sent me $500 on PayPal.

He was so impressed that he turned around and offered me another $1,000 to install the same software on two more sites for him. Yes, sir! Coming right up!

Now the gravy train had really started. I was getting referral after referral. Within a month, I had completed over 20 projects and netted over $10,000 in consulting fees!

That month, I earned a total of $15,000: $10,000 from consulting and $5,000 from my online affiliate commissions.

I had now made in one month what most of my friends would make in 6 months of full time work. You'd think I was excited, right?

Not so much. Remember, I was a full-time student. Between classes, running traffic to my affiliate website, and all of the consulting deals I was getting, I was barely sleeping.

This was **not** the hands-off, autopilot business that I had set out to create. It was out of control.

I knew there was a better way.

Once again, I went out looking for an answer. As I voiced this concern to many of my friends on the forum, someone sent me a superb idea. *(Pay close attention here. This was about to become the Digital Publishing model that has absolutely changed my life ever since.)*

He asked: *"Anik, why are you consulting? You're killing yourself! Why don't you just make a quick video of you installing the software on a website. Make it super step-by-step and just offer that to people for $500. This way they can use the software themselves, you still make $500, and you never have to lift a finger yourself! People will buy it all day long!"*

I remember sitting on this idea for days. It seemed too easy. Would it really work? I decided to give it a try. It would only take me a few hours to make the video course, so I had almost nothing to lose.

I created my first information product (the video course) in less than one day. It was so easy!

I wrote a short message about my new course, took a few pictures of the videos, uploaded them to a new page on my ugly affiliate website, and published it.

Voilà! In about 24 hours my new product was live and ready to be sold. I made a few tweaks to my marketing and went to bed.

You won't believe what happened.

When I logged into my PayPal account the next morning, I had made 4 sales overnight while I slept! That's right. I made $2,000 while I slept. Zero consulting and 100% hands off! It was the quickest and easiest $2,000 I had ever made.

From there, sales just exploded. I started testing some new traffic strategies and by my 4th month in "profit generating" business, I had made $25,000.

I really didn't know what I was doing. I was just testing and trying different things. But my sales never slowed down. Even though I was still only in my third year of college, I was set to make over $300,000 while living the life of my dreams.

I had done it! I had finally discovered the dream business that I had worked so long and so hard to find.

MAKING MONEY HANDS-OFF
MY DREAM BUSINESS

SENT TRAFFIC TO PRODUCT FROM REVIEW PAGE

TESTED NEW TRAFFIC STRATEGIES

CREATED MY 1ST INFORMATION PRODUCT

MADE $2,000 WHILE I SLEPT

MADE $25,000 BY MY 4TH MONTH

HOW I TOOK MY BUSINESS TO $10 MILLION

I had finally discovered the art of selling information on the Internet. Looking back now, I actually chuckle a bit because I was horrible at it. I was making mistake after mistake.

But the business model was so solid that even with my ridiculous mistakes, I was still generating amazing profits. That's when I knew the power of what I had discovered.

There was no turning back for me. I spent the next 45 days building my next information product. Powered with my new expertise in traffic generation and digital publishing, I turned this new information product into an instant bestseller. I used an entirely new traffic source called "affiliate traffic."

I had finally done it. I had found a system that really worked. Not only had I succeeded with it, but many others were quietly creating their own fortunes with this same system. The key was simply to follow the system step-by-step.

I sold thousands of units of my second product. I was still in my last year of college. In fact, I was well on track to generating over $1 million in sales before I even graduated.

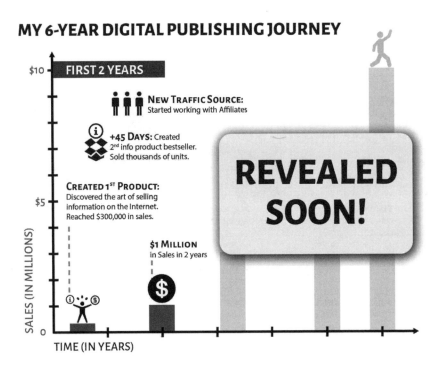

MY 6-YEAR DIGITAL PUBLISHING JOURNEY

$10

FIRST 2 YEARS

NEW TRAFFIC SOURCE: Started working with Affiliates

+45 DAYS: Created 2nd info product bestseller. Sold thousands of units.

CREATED 1ST PRODUCT: Discovered the art of selling information on the Internet. Reached $300,000 in sales.

$5

$1 MILLION in Sales in 2 years

REVEALED SOON!

SALES (IN MILLIONS)

0

TIME (IN YEARS)

I was 100% sold on the digital publishing model by now. But I knew there was still more to this system. I wasn't done learning. Not yet. I wanted more. Remember, I wanted to change the world.

When I started, there was no program to help me follow a step-by-step plan to maximize my profits. I knew that I had to do all my own research and testing. I had to learn everything the hard way. But the future looked so promising that I was happy to do it.

That was when I discovered a new system that I now call the Profit Multiplier. This incredible system allowed me to triple my profits without a single extra visitor.

I didn't have to work harder to get more traffic. I didn't have to invest any more money either. I was able to take my existing visitors and my existing sales and still multiply the profits by more than 300%.

Using the Profit Multiplier, I raised my sales from $1 million to $3 million.

PROFIT MULTIPLIER IN DIGITAL PUBLISHING

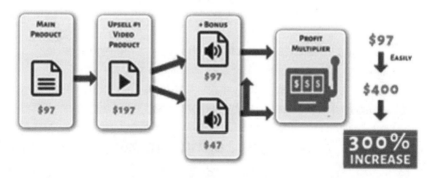

My digital publishing business continued to shock and amaze me. But my inner desire to master, innovate, and scale larger, continued.

I wanted to know what I could do to take my business to $10 million, or even $100 million. I wanted to know how I could take my new business international and build a worldwide empire.

It's important to note here that you have 100% flexibility on how large you want to grow your business. Once you pass the $3 million territory, the business becomes difficult to manage on your own.

This means you have to start hiring employees and becoming a more "formal" business.

For many of my students, this "formal" side of the business is just not their cup of tea. They prefer to live in full freedom, travel the world, and make more than enough to pay for all of it. They opt not to scale into the millions and millions.

That is absolutely ok. It's your business. It's your life. It's your decision.

You decide: What kind of life do you want? My job is simple: To empower and equip you to grow as big as you want.

As I continued researching, testing, and learning, I added more strategies to keep my business growing:

- I added more traffic channels to get more visitors.
- I deepened my use of the Profit Multiplier.
- I used horizontal and vertical expansion to increase my product lineup and niches.
- I deployed affiliate sales to create 100% profit margin revenue.

Using these newfound strategies, it only took me two more years to scale my business to over $10 million in sales per year.

That meant that in only 6 years, I had gone from making $300 in one night to $10 million per year.

During this time, I had won awards from all over the world. I was voted one of the Top 3 Young Entrepreneurs in the United States by *BusinessWeek Magazine*. *Inc 500* rewarded my company as one of the fastest-growing companies in the United States for two years in a row.

Awards like this were coming in from all over the world - all because of information marketing.

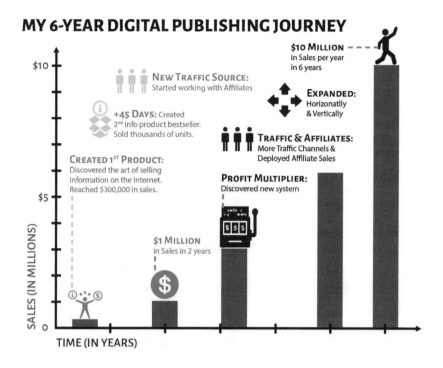

MY 6-YEAR DIGITAL PUBLISHING JOURNEY

In just six years, I had grown a business from $300 a night to now generating over $10 million in sales per year. I was just a kid making mistakes, with no one showing me the ropes. That's how powerful this simple business model is.

I was riding high, and then...I fell into $1.7 Million of debt.

From $300,000 to $1 million. From $1 million to $3 million. From $3 million to $10 million. Then bankrupt.

Yes, you read that right. Bankrupt.

This story is difficult for me to tell. Some of the best days in my life ended up leading me to some of the darkest days of my life.

It actually took me years of healing just to get to a place where I could talk about it. However, I know that there are some great lessons in my "nearly bankrupt" story. I know that if I share these lessons with you, you can save yourself a lot of money, pain, and heartache.

So how did these dark clouds of failure start to hover over me, just when I should have been at the top of the world?

Here's how.

In 2010, I began to grow over-confident. I started to believe that it wasn't the system that was leading my success, but rather it was my own personal genius. I call this my "golden touch" era.

I began to veer away from my business model. I began trying to re-invent a wheel that needed no changes. I started fixing things that didn't need fixing.

300% annual growth wasn't good enough for me anymore. I wanted to see the company hit $1 billion. I wanted to break records.

In my quest for faster growth, I abandoned my proven digital publishing system. I hired unnecessary employees. I built unnecessary offices around the world. I tried to mimic "big" businessmen.

That's what they do in Silicon Valley, right? They get millions of dollars (which I had) and they invest it in fancy offices and more employees. But this new way of running my business came at a major cost. My attention went away from the proven model and became distracted by flash and ego.

When I look back now, it isn't at all surprising that I started to lose money. The wild thing is that the first year that my business actually lost money was the same year that I generated over $10 million in sales. How crazy is that? It still shocks me. How do you generate $10 million in sales and then actually lose money that same year?

By believing everything you touch will turn to gold. By believing that you can abandon the system that got you the $10 million in the first place.

How bad did things get, that fateful year of 2010?

- My health was deteriorating at a dramatic rate.
- Every 3 months, I found myself in a new hospital fighting for my life.
- I nearly died from internal bleeding before a flight home from Amsterdam.
- I was depressed beyond belief.
- I had lost all faith in myself.
- I was $1.7 million in debt. Most of this was owed to close family and friends who had lent me their life savings.
- I had routine panic attacks trying to figure out how I would ever escape this crushing debt.

I owed everyone money, from my parents to friends to multiple banks and credit cards. My phone began to ring every hour, on the hour. There were days when I would find myself hiding. No one would know where I was, not even my own family.

The darkness reached its peak when I had to be carted off of a plane in Amsterdam. The plane was preparing to take off just as a flight attendant found me unconscious in my seat. When I came to, I was on a stretcher on my way to the nearest hospital.

This was my wakeup call. I was in a hospital bed, alone in a foreign land. I was literally tied down with tube after tube. What had happened to me?

When I began my journey, I had one mission: I wanted to find freedom. Yet here I was literally strapped to a bed and weighed down with endless tubing.

This was not freedom.

That's when I decided to drastically change my life. I flew back home and immediately shut down all of my offices. I got rid of most of my 86-person staff. (The reality is that you don't need employees in this business model).

It was time to get back to basics.

It was time to go back to the system that had built my business to begin with. It was time to get back to the top - and this time, stay there. I would never again let greed blind me from the simplicity of the digital publishing business model.

BACK TO $10 MILLION IN JUST 16 MONTHS

The most shocking part of my story? It had taken me 6 years to go from $100 to $10 million. But this time around, I could deploy the same step-by-step system and reach $10 million in just 16 months.

In just 16 months, I paid back every penny of the $1.7 million I owed.

I was full of passion again. I sprang out of bed every morning and leaped at the chance to get work done.

The #1 Lesson I ever learned? Always stick to the system. If you want to build a stress-free, life-changing business, you've got to stick to a system.

If it's working, don't change it. Don't abandon it. Rinse and repeat. Over and over. Scale it as high as the system will allow. Do that, and you'll never have to worry about the kind of bad days I experienced.

Ever since I learned that lesson - and I learned it the hard way - I've made millions of dollars year after year. Ever since that day, I have always kept the digital publishing model as simple as it is meant to be. I stuck with this system exactly as I learned it. My focus now is purely on horizontal and vertical expansion. Sure, I still want to grow my business to new heights.

But I've learned never to abandon the business model system again. Check out this picture of my work desk.

I don't even have an office. I work from home. I travel about 60% of the year and my laptop is more than enough to continue running my empire.

In 2016, my business is on track to genertate over $20 million in sales, and it's easier to manage than ever. All thanks to the beauty and simplicity of the digital publishing system.

I've shared my story so that you could truly understand how much of a blessing the digital publishing business model can be to your life.

But that's enough about me. Let's talk about how you can become an entrepreneur, build the life of your dreams, and do it all using the digital publishing business model.

CASE STUDY: DORI FRIEND
TURNING EXPERTISE INTO MILLIONS [2]

Dori Friend has been an expert in her niche for many years. She came to me just a few months back. Her goal was to increase her authority and influence within her niche. I shared with her my 7-step digital publishing system.

Using her expertise and my system, she created her first information product this year. She went into it with zero expectations.

"I just want to make a dollar," she told me.

How did she do? She far exceeded her expectations, to say the least.

She made more than a million dollars with that one single information product.

Well done, Dori!

---

[2] These results may not be typical nor expected for every person. This is not a "get rich quick" scheme. Your level of success in attaining similar results is dependent upon a number of factors that are not the responsibility of Lurn, Inc. These factors include your skills, ability to follow through, dedication, network, and financial situation, etc.

CHAPTER 2: THE RIGHT TIME

Why is this the right time to start your digital publishing business? You don't have to take my word for it. Just look at the data and you'll see that there has never been a better time than now to start your digital publishing business.

First I'll show you why it's the right time to start an online business versus an offline business. Then we'll discuss the digital publishing business model specifically.

- By 2016, more than 50% of all U.S. retail business will be directly influenced by the Internet. The day of only buying things at the store are fast disappearing. *Source: Forrester Research*

- $592.43 billion. That's the amount that companies invested in online advertising in 2015 alone. If you ever want to see trends in the world of business, just watch where companies are spending their money for advertising. *Source: eMarketer*

- According to a survey of 2,445 US online consumers, 82% considered user-generated reviews to be extremely valuable. *Source: North American Technographics Retail Online*

- Every month there are more than 10.3 billion Google searches, with 78% of U.S. Internet users researching products and services online. The market is clearly now sticking to the Internet to research and find their products. *Source B2B Marketing*

- $304 billion in online sales were generated in 2014 in the U.S. alone. Online businesses are growing year after year at over 15% a year. *Source: eMarketer*

WEB SALES & GROWTH FROM 2005 UNTIL 2015

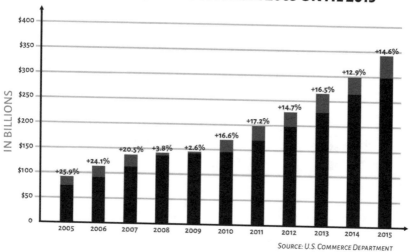

SOURCE: U.S. COMMERCE DEPARTMENT

Let's face it. It's 100% clear that the world is moving to the Internet. If you want to start your own business and make your dreams come true, opening a physical store is no longer the best way. There are hundreds of ways to start making money online.

So why is the digital publishing business model by far the best strategy?

- In 2013, Amazon declared that their digital book sales surpassed their physical book sales. This is an enormous indication of the future of digital publishing.

- $5.5 billion: In 2014, Amazon is estimated to have sold billions in just digital information.

- While traditional bookstores are shutting their doors, digital publishing sales have grown by about $1 billion every year since 2008. This is a clear indication that people are now turning to the Internet for the information they need.

- eBook sales are expected to reach $9.7 billion in 2016. *Source: Forrester Research*

- By 2020, self-published books will outsell traditionally published books. *Source: Suvyati*

- JVZoo.com is a new online platform released just years ago. It has already crossed well over $150 million in digital product sales.

- ClickBank.com, a leader in the digital publishing industry, has produced well over $1 billion in sales.

These are the facts, and they serve as hard proof that we are at the growth explosion of digital information marketing right now. This is absolutely the perfect moment to develop your own product and take full control of your financial future.

THE TOP 5 REASONS DIGITAL PUBLISHING IS CURRENTLY THE BEST WAY TO START YOUR ONLINE BUSINESS

- **Automation** — Set it, forget it, profit.
  From generating traffic to growing your list to converting customers, just about every step in this digital publishing model is automated.

- **Information** — All the content you need.
  People pay good money to learn something of value. Fortunately for you, the Internet is bursting with all the content you'll ever need.

- **Outsourcing** — Let experts do the work for you.
  From writing your content to designing your website to recording your webinar, there are countless experts ready to complete your product quickly and inexpensively.

- **Completely Virtual** — Anytime, anywhere.
  Digital publishing doesn't require a physical space. All you need is a computer and a passion to educate others.

- **Infinitely Scalable** — Grow, Grow, Grow.
  Want to build a bigger list? Want to make more sales? Simply provide more value or offer more digital products. Use horizontal growth or repeat the system in new niches.

There are hundreds of ways to start an online business, but this I guarantee: There isn't a more effective, faster, easier or more proven way than digital publishing.

CHAPTER 3: THE SIMPLICITY

THE 7 SIMPLE STEPS TO LAUNCHING YOUR BUSINESS

Let's learn exactly what it takes to get your business up and running. Check out this diagram:

This really is it. Most of these steps can be broken down into tiny, simple baby steps. All you need to do is follow each step. Before you know it (in a matter of just a few weeks) your business will be live and transacting online.

"Do I need technology skills or other skills?"

Let's get this #1 objection out of the way. Most of the steps you see in this diagram can be automated using existing technology. You do not need to be a technical wizard or a writing genius. Heck, I'm not - and I've sold millions online!

All right. Time to dive in. What exactly are the steps?

STEP #1: NICHE
FIND THE PERFECT NICHE FOR YOU

This is where it gets fun. Start by finding a niche that's primed for awesomeness; one that has a big market and lots of hungry prospects.

You can choose from an almost unlimited number of niches on the Internet. Some niches are big. Some are small. Within each niche, there are usually sub-niches.

Here's a secret few people know: You can make money in almost any niche. You simply have to meet a few criteria that I will show you in just a minute.

I have watched our students succeed in every kind of niche topic you can imagine:

- Knitting... Gold mine!
- Bottle collecting... Jackpot!
- Wine tasting... Superb!
- Personal development... One of my favorites!

The possibilities are truly unlimited.

CASE STUDY: JIMMY KIM
DIGITAL PUBLISHING IGNITED HIS $4 MILLION A YEAR BUSINESS[3]

Jimmy Kim used to work 15+ hour days at a car dealership. Working long, unforgiving hours for little pay, he was about to throw in the towel.

"There HAS to be an easier way," Jimmy would say to himself, "A better way to have more time, more freedom, and more money!"

---

[3] These results may not be typical nor expected for every person. This is not a "get rich quick" scheme. Your level of success in attaining similar results is dependent upon a number of factors that are not the responsibility of Lurn, Inc. These factors include your skills, ability to follow through, dedication, network, and financial situation, etc.

When Jimmy and I became friends, he had no clue what this world of digital publishing was all about. He couldn't grasp its immense potential.
Still, I trained him using my proven step-by-step digital publishing system. His goal for his very first product launch was modest: He wanted to make just a few thousand dollars.

He did just that - and then some: He sold **$82,000 worth!**

Jimmy was flat out shocked. Yes, he had always been a good provider for his family, but that one launch completely altered his perspective. He beamed with pride as he talked about what his new income meant to his family and how proud they were of him.

Today, Jimmy rakes in $4 million a year. His life has been completely transformed.

Jimmy went from working crazy hours, selling cars nonstop, and being stressed all the time to living a more fulfilling life and enjoying the vast freedom of being a millionaire entrepreneur.

He was able to turn this corner because he allowed me to show him an easier way - a proven model for digital publishing.

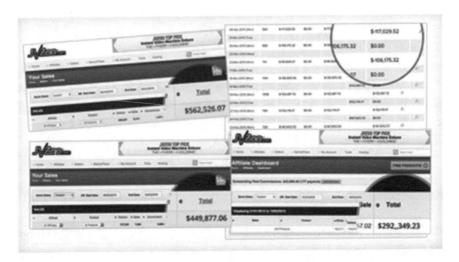

HOW TO FIND YOUR OWN PERFECT NICHE

So where do you start?

That's easy. You start in your own heart.

Look at your own expertise, passions, and hobbies. I call this the E.P.H. approach to building the life of your dreams. First, make a list of possible topics. Then, filter those ideas through certain criteria.

Think for a moment:

- Where do you enjoy spending your time?
- What are you especially good at?
- What is the one topic that your friends always seek advice from you on?

That's where you start.

Why? Because my own research and studies overwhelmingly prove that when you choose a niche that really lights a fire in you personally, you're 10 times more likely to succeed.

It makes sense. If you don't like to cook, you are not going to enjoy a digital publishing business built around cooking. Any niche you don't personally enjoy is eventually going to feel like drudgery - and you'll be building the business for all the wrong reasons.

If your passion is golfing, you would have a blast building an entire business around golfing, wouldn't you? It would feel a lot like you were getting paid to do something that you love. That's our goal – to give you that feeling.

Now, is a passion for your niche enough on its own?

No. Definitely not.

If you want to launch a business, make more money, and enjoy more freedom and opportunity, you need to first research the competition in your possible niche.

Mark my words: If you cannot find other information marketers who are already selling in your proposed niche, run for your life. Do not choose that niche.

Believe me. You want competition. Competition is excellent for your niche potential.

Now let's assume your research has revealed that yes, indeed, competition exists in several of your E.P.H. list's niche choices. Here's how to proceed. It's easy.

FREE ONLINE NICHE EVALUATION TOOLS

Use the following tools - all free and readily available online - to finish evaluating your specific niche.

1. **Amazon.com**
   Use Amazon to review existing information on competitive products that are being sold.

2. **Facebook Ads Platform**
   Facebook has an amazing analysis tool, and you don't need to spend a dime to use it.

3. **Clickbank.com**
   This is one of my favorite sources to see if a particular niche is selling well or not.

4. **Google Keywords Tool**
   Get a quick glance for free on the popularity of the biggest keywords in your niche.

In addition to these free online tools, here's my own 5 Point Checklis that I've developed over my years in the industry. This checklist will help you to determine whether you're on track with a great niche that's going to be both profitable and long-lasting.

5 POINT CHECKLIST TO DETERMINE A GOOD NICHE

1. Is it possible to create digital information products in this niche?

2. Are there competing offers in this niche that are already making money?

3. Is it cost-feasible to advertise to this niche?

4. Are the customers in this niche motivated strongly by emotion?

5. Is it scalable for the long term?

These are critical questions when it comes to the success of your product. If you can answer "yes" to some, but not all, of these points, you probably need to narrow your niche slightly, or rethink your angle to make sure its appeal is unique.

However, if you can answer "yes" to each of the 5 points above, you'll never have to worry about launching a business in a "risky" niche.

STEP #2: YOUR OWN INFORMATION PRODUCT
BRING YOUR KNOWLEDGE AND EXPERIENCE TO LIFE

The top 3 objections I hear from my newest students (who go on to become ragingly successful if they listen to me) are:

Objection 1: I'm not a writer; I don't know how to create a product.

Objection 2: I don't know anything worth teaching anyone.

Objection 3: How do I put together a course? I don't know anything about teaching!

These objections are actually excuses, and they're based in fear. I know, because I used to say them. I often hear these fear-based objections/ excuses from people who are in the same place as I was when I started.

But if I've said it once, I'll say it again: You don't have to be afraid, and you can stop making excuses. Here's why:

- **I'm not a writer.** In fact, writing was my worst subject in school. One of my teachers literally said to me: "Anik, you'll never be a writer." (I made sure she was the first person who received my first course 11 years ago!)

- **I'm an expert, but for years I never knew it.** The truth is this. If you have spent months or years immersing yourself in any field or topic, you truly possess a great deal of information that others will find tremendously valuable.

- **I had no idea how to create an online course.** I was 100% lost - the last person in the world who would know how to put together an online course. Once I saw the system to do it, I finally understood how simple it could be. You can copy that very same template.

I've distilled this system down to a science. But you don't have to take my word for it. I've watched thousands of my students overcome their objections and do this. Many of my personal friends use this same system and build amazing businesses.

CASE STUDY: RITOBAN CHAKRABARTI
FROM SMALL TOWN IN INDIA TO MILLIONAIRE [4]

Meet Ritoban. He was just like many college kids from rural towns in India. When he graduated, his reward would be a salary of just $300-$350 a month - barely enough to live.

He knew there had to be a better way. So he tried digital publishing. He started out doing pretty well, but wanted more. He wanted to make a name for himself throughout India. He wanted it so badly that he could practically taste the success.

---

[4] These results may not be typical nor expected for every person. This is not a "get rich quick" scheme. Your level of success in attaining similar results is dependent upon a number of factors that are not the responsibility of Lurn, Inc. These factors include your skills, ability to follow through, dedication, network, and financial situation, etc.

Inspired by his passion and drive, I took him under my wing. Ritoban was so appreciative. He was so thankful for the time I spent working with him.

I put him through the same 7-step process that you're starting to learn, but Ritoban had more challenges than many of my students; perhaps more than you.

English was his second language. His dial-up Internet connection was very slow.

It didn't matter to Ritoban. Every challenge he faced became another opportunity to prove himself to his family, his friends, and even me.

I still remember every one of his major milestones: When he made his first $10,000. When he made his first $100,000. And yes, when he made his first MILLION dollars online! Like a little boy who just scored the winning goal, Ritoban ran through the streets sharing his great news with all of his loved ones.

What I love most about Ritoban is that he has never lost his enthusiasm. He appreciates the opportunity he has been given, and he puts all of his energy into his digital publishing business.

In just 4 years, he's done over $4 million in sales - with English as his second language, with an Internet connection that crawled slowly, and with poverty as far as the eye can see.

Keep it up, Ritoban! You're making India proud!

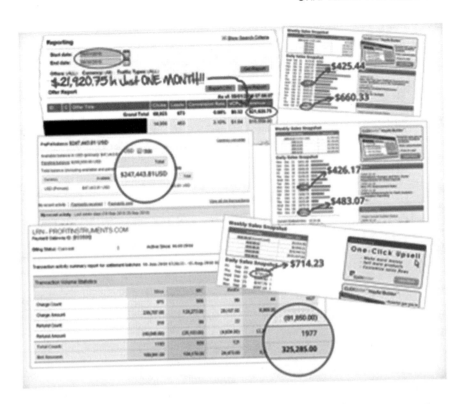

You don't need to be a writer. You don't need to know anything about technology. You don't need to be highly educated. You don't even need to be a traditional "expert" at anything! Keep this - and Ritoban's story - in mind whenever you find yourself coming up with objections and excuses.

THE 5 LEVEL PROGRESSION TO CREATE YOUR INFORMATION PRODUCT

Now that we've eliminated any objections or excuses you might have about taking the plunge into digital publishing, let's look at the 5 key steps you need to take in order to create your very own valuable information product.

1. **Research** existing information products.

2. **Discover** your unique angle.

3. **Decide** on your choice of media: Written, audio, or video product.

4. Create a product outline.

5. Assign responsibility and create a timeline. Will you create the product or will you get some help?

It's important to go through these 5 levels in order, from your initial research to actually creating your product. That's why we're going to look at each level in more detail next.

PRODUCT CREATION LEVEL 1: RESEARCH EXISTING INFORMATION PRODUCTS

In Step #1, you went through a methodical process to choose the right niche for you. You started with your own passion and interests, and then filtered them down using the free online niche evaluation tools listed as well as my 5 Point Checklist.

Before you start creating your own product, you need to dig a little deeper into your niche by doing a little legal spy work. If you haven't already, find at least 5 products in the niche you've chosen. That's easy - just do a quick Google search using your niche keywords and pick 5 different products. (Remember, if your niche doesn't have plenty of competing products already, you've chosen the wrong niche.)

Now go through each of those sales funnels as if you were a customer. Knowing exactly how your competition is selling their products will help you to determine what is working and what isn't - especially when it comes to creating your own products. Are they using written sales letters? Ebooks? Audiobooks? Video sales letters? Webinars? Online courses? Which products stand out as successful, and why?

Carefully dissect each of your competing niche products. Find out what's working and figure out why. I guarantee you'll go about choosing and creating your own product more wisely and effectively after you've done this bit of spying on your competition.

PRODUCT CREATION LEVEL 2:
DISCOVER YOUR UNIQUE ANGLE

At this point it's important to start thinking about your product's unique angle. The unique angle is what makes customers find your product more enticing than your competitor's product. You could be offering the very same product at the very same price - but if your angle is well-crafted, your customers will click your "Buy Now" button, not your competitor's.

Your angle is based on your Unique Selling Proposition, or USP, along with your product's unique "hook." Your USP tells your customers why your product is the better choice. It answers their question: "Why should I care about this?" or "What's this going to do for me?" For example, if you're offering a Paleo diet ebook, your USP might be something like "The Paleo Diet That Feels Like You're Not On A Diet."

Your hook, on the other hand, puts your USP into terms that your customers will understand quickly - and hooks them, often emotionally. You can often use your hook right in your advertising as a headline or a subhead. The hook for our Paleo USP might be something like: "Are you tired of feeling like you're missing out on great food when you diet?" It taps into your customer's feeling about Paleo diets, and sounds pretty enticing, doesn't it?

PRODUCT CREATION LEVEL 3:
DECIDE ON YOUR CHOICE OF MEDIA

This is a major stage in the product creation process, so I've developed a methodical approach to help choose the type of media you will create: Written, Audio, or Video. Each of these offers several different product options. But first, you need to consider:

1. What is the price of your product?

Choosing a desired price point will determine what kind of product type you will need to create.

2. Do you like writing? Are you shy? Are you OK with recording audio or video?

At this point we examine some of your personal choices. There is never a right or wrong answer here. Your business will mold to your preferences.

3. Are you willing to get some outside help to create your information product?

There's a world of outsourcers who are experts in their field. These outsourcers can help you create parts of your product or most of it. Investing in this is 100% up to you. If you are willing to make a small investment, options do open up!

THE 3 PRODUCT TYPES

1. Written Product
2. Audio Product
3. Video Product

Each of these 3 product types are rockstar successes online. Here's what to consider when making your choice:

WRITTEN PRODUCTS

Digital written products come in many forms. They can be as simple as an eBook, or they can be offered as a course by splitting them into several parts. Many times, the way you present your information can dramatically increase the monetary value of your product.

Remember, you don't have to write or create the product yourself. You can always use outsourcers to help you create your written product - and you may be surprised at their affordability.

AUDIO PRODUCTS

Although an audio product is a step above a written product, it can be as simple as an audiobook. You might also opt to structure your audio product as an audio course series - using the very same audio files.

Creating an audio product is similar to creating a written product. The only difference is that you will grab an inexpensive microphone and some free audio software to record yourself reading the written word. Don't want to be the one reading it? No problem. You can outsource amazing voice-over talent to record the audio for you, inexpensively of course.

There are various kinds of audio products, many ways to create them, and they're not difficult at all. Choose whichever type of audio product fits your personality best:

- **Straight Recording**
  Is your head packed with information? Then go straight to recording. I love doing this! I have a clip-on microphone ($35 at a local store). I plug it into my phone or a hand-held audio recorder. I walk around my room and simply talk about various topics. Within a couple of hours, I have a Class A product completed and packed with valuable information.

- **Script & Read**
  Need some help? Do you feel more comfortable being prepared with a script? That's simple too. First, create a written product. Then simply record yourself reading it.

- **Interview Experts**
  Let others do the work for you. Download Skype (it's free). Then download a quick audio recording software. Now line up some interviews with existing experts in your niche and record them. Done.

By now you should be starting to understand that if you can open your mind and follow my system, you can very easily create your own digital information product - without being a college professor!

VIDEO PRODUCTS

This type of product carries the highest perceived value, but it also comes with the greatest misconceptions. Every time I suggest that a student create a video product, I hear something like this in response: "I hate video cameras! I can't make videos! That's for experts!"

I laugh and ask them, "What if you can make a video product worth hundreds or even thousands of dollars without ever showing your face in front of a camera?"

That's usually when their eyes light up. There are many ways to create a Class A video product because there are many different styles of video:

- **Create Screen-Capture Video**
  This is simply recording your computer screen. For example, you can create and record a PowerPoint presentation or a live demonstration of anything you want. You never have to show your face on camera.

- **Conduct Webinar Interviews**
  This is a strategy to create a video product that does both things for you. One, you never have to show your face on camera. Two, you don't even have to create the content yourself. You simply do a webinar interview with existing experts.

- **Run Your Own Webinar Series**
  Create a series of PowerPoint files around the topics you want to teach. Then turn on your screen capture recording tool, hit "record," and walk your listeners through your PowerPoints while speaking into a microphone.

Congratulations! You now have a very high value educational course.

- **Create a Face to Camera Video**
  Face to Camera Videos carry the highest value, plus you get a chance to build a relationship with your students. But please note that you don't have to do this until you're comfortable with the idea and the process.

CHAPTER 3: THE SIMPLICITY

ODD NICHE? NOT AN EXPERT? HERE'S ONE STUDENT'S ADVICE

Ever heard of crochet? Until Ty Cohen explained it was a needlepoint craft, I had never heard of it. And I certainly didn't think there was a viable market for it.

It turns out there IS a viable market - and it's at least six figures big! That's what Ty has made using my digital publishing system to launch his how-to crochet digital product.

The best part? Ty knows very little about crochet. He'll be the first to tell you he's not an expert by any means. Yet he can still create an information product loaded with value that people happily buy.

He did the same thing in the Fiction Novelist niche. He built a multiple six figure business with almost no professional credibility.

Here's what Ty says:

> *"If I could offer advice to those out there who don't consider themselves experts or who aren't sure which niche to get into, I'd say just get started. Don't wait. Find a niche you like, do a little research, and follow Anik's steps. You'll be amazed with the finished product... and results!"*
> - Ty Cohen

Isn't it shocking to learn how easy all this can be? Your written, audio, or video product will be professional, polished, and jam-packed with valuable information. No matter what your experience level is. No matter where you are in your life, you can and will have your own digital information product.

PRODUCT CREATION LEVEL 4:
CREATE A PRODUCT OUTLINE

No matter what your niche is, no matter what type of product you're going to create, no mater if you will outsource the creation of your product, your product outline is your first step in product creation, and it's going to make the entire process much simpler and less stressful.

Your product outline is not only fun to do, but it will keep you focused and result in a far better product. Creating your product outline is one of the most enjoyable, easy parts of digital publishing - at least it's one of my favorite parts of the process. I've never once created any product without first writing up a product outline. It's easy.

Here's how: Get a whiteboard or a piece of paper and start brainstorming all the various things you are going to cover in this product. Don't worry about writing them down in order, and don't worry (for now) if one thing is more important than another. Just get it all down on paper in a list.

Once you've written down everything, take a step back and put them in the order you think makes the most sense and will make the product topic the most understandable for your customers. This sorted list will represent your chapter titles if you're doing an ebook, interview topics if you're doing an audio product which features an expert, class titles if you're doing an online course - you get the picture.

Next, you start to break each item down into its own sub-topics. Sub-topics can be broken down even further into their own sub-topics. Continue to fill in the information and gaps and you will slowly start to see that your product is being created right before your own eyes. Whether you turn this into a slideshow, video, or any other product, you now have a professional-caliber product that covers your topic in a full and organized manner.

If you're outsourcing the product, your outline will save you time, money and aggravation because it shows your outsourcer exactly what you want and in what order.

PRODUCT CREATION LEVEL 5: ASSIGN RESPONSIBILITY AND CREATE A TIMELINE

You've done your research. You've crafted a unique angle. You've chosen the perfect medium, and you've written up your outline. Now it's time to assign responsibility and to create your product timeline so everything stays on track.

Your timeline can be as simple as making a list of the various elements of your product creation and assigning deadlines for each item. If you're creating a video course, for example, you'll want to include deadlines for elements like creating the PowerPoint slides and shooting the screen-capture video.

Breaking your production into chunks which you can cross off a list will keep you organized and feeling like you're truly accomplishing something. It's also the only way to be sure you don't spend your time on re-perfecting a product that was ready to go months ago.

Finally, you'll need to decide whether you're going to create your product by yourself or whether you'll get some help. Outsourcing does incur expense but you'll be amazed at how small that expense can be when you use online platforms which offer a wide choice of deadline-oriented talent from around the world.

Making this decision is a little easier when you can visualize your end product. What do you want your product to look like, sound like, and feel like to your customer? Can you realistically produce that by yourself? It's very possible that you can. On the other hand, you may be able to do most of the work - conceptualizing, organizing, researching, and writing - but you need someone to polish up the language, handle graphic, or deal with other aspects of your production.

Just remember, you can outsource a tiny portion of your job, a good deal of it, or the whole thing. Either way, outsourcing can be a lot easier and less expensive than you might think.

Once your product creation is under way, it's time to look at Step #3 in our 7-Step diagram:

STEP #3: THE PROFIT MULTIPLIER

Once you've decided on your niche and your product type, it's time to look at maximizing your profits. Doing this is a lot easier than most people realize. For example, the following simple "funnel" can instantly raise your income by 300% or more:

You: "I'll take a Big Mac"

Cashier: "Do you want fries with that?"

You: "Sure."

Cashier: "How about a soda as well? It's only another dollar."

You: "OK! Why not?"

In this example, you just spent about 300% more than you had initially planned. On the other hand, you probably feel better served, more satisfied, and happier with your purchase.

You can create this identical process online with digital publishing. Actually, it's even easier with digital publishing - and it's more powerful. Keep on reading and I will teach you the strategy of "funnels."

FUNNELS

There are two kinds of funnels: The At Cart Funnel and the Back End Funnel.

1. At Cart Funnel

The Big Mac dialog above is a great example of the At Cart Funnel. It's when you strategically make additional offers to your customer right as they are in the process of buying the initial product.

AT CART FUNNEL

Big Mac	Fries	Coke			
$3.99	$1.79	$1.49			

2. Back End Funnel

The Back End Funnel is a very specific follow-up plan that lasts for weeks after you get your first customer. It's one of the easiest ways to radically impact the profitability of your business.

Do you need to be a skilled sales person to build sales funnels? No.

There is a very specific science to a funnel, but the technology to implement it is 100% automated. Great funnel builders consider several different types of sales, and I'm going to make you a master of them all:

- **Main Offer Downsell**
  97-99% of the people who visit your website will leave without ever buying a single thing. This is just the harsh reality and it's virtually impossible to avoid, but it does not mean that you have to let them go forever. To capture as much value from these visitors as possible, I will teach you strategies that will guarantee at least 40-50% of the traffic you get will take at least some action.

- **At Cart Upsell**
  This is the quickest and easiest way to double your profits without ever getting a single extra visitor to your website.

- **At Cart Downsell**

  Add another 50% to your sales by adding one simple page into your sales process. Again, this can be 100% automated.

- **Back End Upsell**

  Within 30 days of getting a new customer, I am able to see a minimum of 100-150% increase in my profits simply by using my easy-to-master back end formula.

- **Back End Affiliate Promotion**

  What if you could make hundreds of thousands of dollars while better serving your customers - and never lifting a finger? This is precisely what I will teach you here.

YES, YOU DO HAVE A SUCCESSFUL PRODUCT WITHIN YOU!

Here's the proof:

"Yes, you can do this!" I don't know how many times I said this to my friend, Jon Talarico. But no matter how many times I said it, he just didn't believe it. He thought you had to be a genuine teacher or certified expert to create an information product.

Hogwash! I finally convinced Jon to try my easy step-by-step system. "Trust the system," I told him. He finally did, and he finished his entire course in just a matter of weeks! His product? Simply amazing! In fact, I challenge any "true expert" to create something better.

"I was the one person who never thought I'd have a digital product within me. However, by following Anik's amazing steps, I've created a program I'm super proud of. Even better, people who buy my product absolutely love it!"

- Jon Talarico

Are you starting to see that bringing your knowledge and experience to life, offering it as a digital product, and marketing it is easier than you think? Using my proven 7-step system and powerful sales funnel strategies can make the process easy and profitable too.

Now let's talk a bit about how to deliver your product to your market.

STEP #4: DELIVERY
DELIVERY OF YOUR CONTENT

Once your product is created (this can be done in just a matter of days if you want) and you have a beautiful 3x funnel created, what's next?

Now it's time to get your awesome product into the hands of your hungry market! This is where some students get a bit antsy. Why? Because this is the first step which involves technology.

Listen, I've been an online entrepreneur for over a decade now, and I still can't put up a webpage for the life of me - much less a members area for a product.

Why am I telling you this? Because it does not matter! You do not need to know anything about technology to get a beautiful product up and running. When I started over a decade ago, my choices were to either learn how to do it on my own (not a chance) or spend a small fortune hiring someone else to get it done.

That was 14 years ago. Today, we're in a very different world. You can either:

- **Outsource it** - Hire someone to help you for **far less** than you think.

- **Automate it** - This is my favorite. For next to nothing, you can now use amazing technology to build your entire business. Just click a few buttons and you're up and running in only hours. You don't have to learn programming, hosting, or anything technical. The systems that are available in today's marketplace do it all for you.

Today, getting your course up and running online is almost too easy! It's literally the easiest part of the process. Believe me. I know so little about technology, yet I can put up an entire members area in a matter of hours today if I need to. And so can you.

STEP #5: MESSAGING
THE SIMPLE SHORTCUT THAT TURNS PROSPECTS INTO PROFITABLE CUSTOMERS

Once you have created your product, funnel, and classroom, it's time to get the attention of your prospects. More specifically, you won't only get their attention, but you will get them to take action. This action means you get to start creating profit, and it's done through your sales messaging.

Sales messaging is where prospects become customers. It's where you begin to build toward your dream of financial freedom.

Please don't let the word "sales" intimidate you. You're not meeting with people face-to-face. You're not even talking to them on the phone. You're simply following a proven methodical step-by-step system to create one of the following items:

The 3 Key Messaging Tools

I have personally used each of these 3 sales messaging tools to sell millions of dollars worth of products online.

1. **Written Sales Letter:** A web page which features a letter written to convince visitors to buy your product.

2. **Video Sales Letter (VSL):** A web page featuring a recorded video in which you (or an outsourced voice over talent) convince visitors to buy your product.

3. **Webinar:** This is a live online seminar in which you provide information for vieweres and at the same time convince them to buy

your product. A webinar can also be recorded and used in a non-live scenario.

It's important to note that each of these sales messaging tools follow a very simple system and template.

Each offers its own advantages and disadvantages based on the positioning, audience, offer, and price. Don't worry. Choosing the right one for you can be done in minutes as it all depends on the price point you'll choose for your product.

STEP #6: IGNITION LAUNCH
RELEASE YOUR PRODUCT & CREATE YOUR FIRST $10,000 IN SALES!

Let me ask you a silly question. When NASA launched decades ago, do you think the scientists sat down and immediately said: "All right guys, let's land on the moon. Actually, forget the moon. Let's go land on Mars."

No. They didn't. As a matter of fact, when they sat down initially, the only thing they spoke about was how to develop a rocket strong enough to get them into outer space.

After that, they went one goal at a time. And one day, they landed on the moon.

If NASA went one goal at a time, tell me this: Why do I constantly see new online marketers trying to do major "big bang" launches right out of the gate when they first start?

And why do I also see so many potentially great digital marketers wringing their hands and refusing to take even the first step of action because they're waiting for the perfect moment to do their "million dollar launch."

Both of these make my blood boil. Both are the worst ways to approach your business.

Every single one of my most successful students - myself included - have first done what I call an Ignition Launch. We build slowly and move from there. The Ignition Launch lets you create a stress-free environment in which to follow the step-by-step system, and to do it right.

When I entered the personal development niche, I didn't just want to jump into it. I used a very methodical approach when entering the niche and my efforts paid off handsomely. Here's how:

FUTURE OF WEALTH

Everyone who knows me now thinks I'm a natural born Internet Marketer, and that this field has always been my passion. Want to know a secret? For as long as I can remember, I've wanted to make it big in the personal development niche. While my friends in high school were reading about sports and fantasy, I was reading personal development books.

It was my true passion, but I never did anything about it until I was down and out in debt a few years back. Yes, I'm talking about the same dark time that I described to you earlier. I learned then that the best way to help myself was to genuinely help others. So I made myself a promise:

> "When I climb out of debt and depression, I will publish my first personal development product on how I saved my wealth and my life."

When I finally erased my debt and made millions once again, it was time to make good on my promise. I sat down that night and created my 7-step system.

Little did I know that this 7-step system would become the preeminent solution for successful digital publishers worldwide. It only took a couple of weeks to put my entire personal development course together; it just poured out of me!

I called it "Future of Wealth" because I believed that it promised just that. I was so proud of this product! Not only was it a product in the personal development niche that I had created all by myself from scratch. It was also the culmination of my life story. I was essentially putting my life out there for the world to see!

It was also time to test the methodology that we teach. Sure, I thought my product was amazing, but what would the personal development market think?

My tests converted well, so I was ready to do my first Ignition Launch. I had just invented Ignition Launches, and my goal was to make $10,000. To be honest though, I would have been happy making just a couple of thousand.

When the sales totals started rolling in, my jaw dropped. I made $52,000!

Now, this wasn't my first rodeo. While $52K got me jazzed, what really got me excited was knowing the potential my digital information product had! I immediately implemented the Profit Multiplier we covered earlier in Step #3. When I did, I attracted more affiliates and fine-tuned the sales process.

I'll admit that it took me a bit longer than anticipated to set up my business. Why? I was distracted. I was still afraid of falling into debt. Plus, I was entering a niche that was new for me.

During the last 30 days of a 90-day period, I had made $52,000 in sales. Then there was a miraculous turn when I deployed my Profit Multiplier. In the next 6 weeks, Future of Wealth did $1 million in sales! I was amazed!

The following year, I launched the same exact product once again. I made $1 million again!

$4,995.00	Future of Wealth - LIVE EVENT (Early Bird Link)
$117,467.00	Future of Wealth 2.0: 15 Day Accelerator Program
$24,111.00	Future of Wealth 2.0: 15 Day Accelerator Program *SPECIAL $50 OFF*
$33,189.00	Future of Wealth 2.0: Power Habit Transformer
$8,050.00	Future of Wealth 2.0: Power Habit Transformer *SPECIAL $30 OFF*
$200,784.00	Future of Wealth 2.0 - 97% Discount
$678,224.00	Future of Wealth 2.0: The ELITE Inner Circle - $1,791 Free Bonuses
$31,894.00	Future of Wealth 2.0 - *VERY SPECIAL DISCOUNT*

Future of Wealth Total: $1,098,714.00

That's $1 million from a $37 product that I created myself from scratch. For every facet of this product and launch, I used my proven step-by-step digital publishing system. It worked flawlessly.

Here's the bottom line. I don't care what the "guru" marketers say about it. Launches are amazing. Launches can truly propel your business. Launches create brands. The key is to do your launch the right way.

Is It Really Possible To Generate Your First $10,000 QUICKLY?

There is no better way to answer this question than by telling you one more amazing story.

CASE STUDY: WILLIE LANEY
$10,000 IN SALES IN HIS FIRST MONTH ONLINE[5]

Willie Laney has been my assistant for over two years.

He didn't simply learn my digital publishing system, he immersed himself in it so he could help teach it to others.

As he watched student after student change their incomes and lives, he asked himself, "I'm no different than them. Why don't I apply this system to my own life? I can do this!"

He did it. And he did it crazy fast. The day he picked his niche, you would think he just won the lottery. He called me and practically screamed his passion through the phone!

Willie knew that this was more than just a niche. This was going to become his livelihood. He knew that the world was going to begin to see him as an expert in his very own passion niche.

To say he was determined would be an understatement! His first 30 days were spent setting up his business. Then it was time to unleash it into the world. Over the next 30 days, he deployed his Ignition Launch.

In less than 60 days, he completed the entire system start to finish. He picked his niche, created his product, built his members area, completed his messaging, got his funnel done, and launched his product.

I was with him as the sales came in. When his sales reached $500, his face lit up! He told me he felt huge relief that people accepted his product. They accepted him as an expert!

When his sales climbed to $1,000, he was so excited that he didn't know

---

[5] These results may not be typical nor expected for every person. This is not a "get rich quick" scheme. Your level of success in attaining similar results is dependent upon a number of factors that are not the responsibility of Lurn, Inc. These factors include your skills, ability to follow through, dedication, network, and financial situation, etc.

who to tell first. I think he called just about everyone in his phone. I knew the totals would jump even higher, and sure enough they did!

$2,500... $5,000... $7,500! Before long, Willie had made over $10,000. With his FIRST digital product and in his FIRST month online!

Today, Willie is far more than an assistant. He's a leader, a teacher... an expert!

Willie's story is one of my favorites. He overcame his fears and setback, set his mind to focus on the 7 steps, and came out $10,000 richer in one month.

Many people, however, want more than only financial independence; they want to have an impact on the world. Dr. Ted Morter is one of those people. Read now about how he not only dramatically increased his income but also was able to spread his positive messages of healing worldwide.

TESTIMONIAL: HE WANTED TO INFLUENCE THE WORLD. HE DID JUST THAT.[6]

Dr. Ted Morter wasn't your average chiropractor. His practice utilized healing energy. With a successful practice, Dr. Ted came to me with a mission beyond making money: He wanted to influence the world with his energy healing practice.

The problem was that he had never published anything in his life. He didn't even know where to start. I showed him my system, and suddenly, he didn't have to worry about the technical part or even the creative part. My system practically created his digital product for him!

Dr. Ted's first digitally published product brought in over six figures! Today, he's currently launching his third product and watching his business — and his influence — grow exponentially!

"Everyday I'm in awe over how you can spread your message and touch the world with nothing more than a computer and a desire. My message connects with people worldwide."

- Dr. Ted Morter

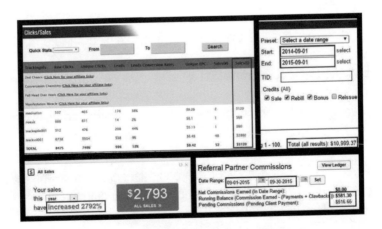

---

[6] These results may not be typical nor expected for every person. This is not a "get rich quick" scheme. Your level of success in attaining similar results is dependent upon a number of factors that are not the responsibility of Lurn, Inc. These factors include your skills, ability to follow through, dedication, network, and financial situation, etc.

STEP #7: GROWTH
SCALE YOUR BUSINESS INTO A MILLION DOLLAR EMPIRE

Up to this step, we've been building your business piece by piece. Now, you're ready to attach a 500-horsepower engine to your business and blast it to a whole new dimension. This is where you start to build a massive brand and become a known name in your niche.

You will begin to have true followers and fans.

- Thousands upon thousands of people following you on email...
- Thousands tracking your every move on social media...
- Hundreds of key relationships – promoters, affiliates, vendors – and everyone will be dying to work with you...
- A growing, scaling business – month after month.

This is where we're going to take your business from doing peanuts ($10,000 per month) to doing millions. Step #7 is when you can quit your day job and take full control of your financial future and your own freedom.

This is also where you will master several proven strategies that can scale your profits by:

- Building relationships by becoming a dominating affiliate marketer in your niche.
- Building traffic to increase daily sales using a completely free traffic generating source.
- Building a lasting brand that's supported by multiple sources of traffic.
- Leveraging your email list to legally begin "printing" money!

This is when it's time to plan your "big bang" launch. This is when we start talking about you doing a $1 million launch and changing the entire financial future of your family in a matter of days.

One of my best student success stories of 2015 is currently enjoying life at Step #7. His story will shock and amaze you.

CASE STUDY: FRED LAM[7]
TRUSTED MY SYSTEM TO THE TUNE OF $1.5 MILLION (AND GROWING)

Fred Lam has been an expert in his niche for over 11 years. For two years, I tried everything I could to convince him to create his own digital information product.

He refused. Even though he was one of the top go-to people in his field, he still didn't think he was credible enough to publish a digital product. I had to practically dare him to publish his expertise.

Finally, he put his fears aside and followed my system to a T. He started marketing his product in February 2015.

Though he put everything he had into his digital product, I just knew there was a small part of him that expected it to fail. Deep down, he didn't really believe that people would buy his product.

What if they didn't value his knowledge? That would crush him.

Despite all of his doubts, his launch was a tremendous success! **By October - in only 8 months - he had already done about $1.5 Million in sales!**

All his hard work and energy had culminated into a huge win — not just financially, but for his confidence as well. Now Fred had great pride in the value he brought to his followers. He knew that from this point forward, nothing could stop him.

Fred expects his projected annual sales this year to be around $2 Million! He just seems like a new man - happier, more outgoing, and simply loving life. Just take a peek at his awesome income proofs.

---

[7] These results may not be typical nor expected for every person. This is not a "get rich quick" scheme. Your level of success in attaining similar results is dependent upon a number of factors that are not the responsibility of Lurn, Inc. These factors include your skills, ability to follow through, dedication, network, and financial situation, etc.

Sales By Date: Monthly					

Date From 4/1/2015 **Date To** 9/30/2015 [Submit]

Month ▾	Orders Count ⇕	Gross Sales ⇕	Shipping ⇕	Taxes ⇕	Net Sales ⇕
April 2015	449	$450653.00	$0.00	$0.00	$450653.00
May 2015	4	$3988.00	$0.00	$0.00	$3988.00
June 2015	4	$5488.00	$0.00	$0.00	$5488.00
July 2015	9	$12973.00	$0.00	$0.00	$12973.00
August 2015	204	$195388.00	$0.00	$0.00	$195388.00
September 2015	228	$156316.00	$0.00	$0.00	$156316.00
Grand Total	**898**	**$824806.00**	**$0.00**	**$0.00**	**$824806.00**

"I owe my digital publishing business success all to Anik and his system. Anik is definitely the best industry-leading expert when it comes to digital publishing."

– Fred Lam

Moving into Step #7, we will focus on 5 key areas to experience a jaw-dropping level of growth.

1. **Build your email list.**

   Your list size = Your business size. If you want to grow, grow your list!

2. **Promote affiliate products.**

   There are experts in your niche with monster lists. There's nothing wrong with creating a profit alongside them, all while serving your list.

3. **Learn Event Based Marketing.**

   This one strategy alone has created millions in profit for me, whether I used it to promote affiliate products or my own. I recently used this strategy to generate over $11.4 million in about 10 days. This strategy is fully based around webinars and works best once you have a 10,000+ name email list.

4. **Horizontal & Vertical Expansion.** Create more of your own products. There is no easier way to add zeros to the end of your revenue numbers than by simply creating more of your own products and repeating this system.

Remember all those people on your list? They signed up for you. Your content, your stories, your products. They are far more likely to buy from you than from your affiliates.

5. **Use Relationships & Networking To Build Your Affiliate Database.**
   The more big affiliates know you and promote your business, the more other affiliates and customers will swarm to you. Make it a priority to get your name out there in the most lucrative affiliate circles.

Does growth happen overnight? Of course not. But if you commit yourself to these 5 key areas, you'll see everything grow right before your eyes.

- Your list will grow.
- Your customer base will grow.
- Your relationships will grow.
- Your confidence will grow.
- Your sales will grow.
- Your profits will grow.

Everything.

But your first mission is to start your business. You've got to get started finding your perfect niche, creating your product, and building a following.

CHAPTER 4: THE SUCCESS

FACT: Only the Action Takers Will Reach Their Dreams

Congratulations! You are among an elite 10% of people who got this book and read all the way to this point.

I have to say I'm very proud of you because very few get this far. It shows me that you are dead serious about your financial future.

But your journey has only just begun. I want to share everything I know with you, but I need you to take action now and graduate into the Top 5%.

How do you graduate into that Top 5%? Becoming a member of that exclusive group is simple, and it will not cost you a penny.

The decision is yours. Are you one of those willing to put in the time and effort to significantly change their lives? Do you really want a business you can call your own? Do you truly want the kind of freedom and opportunity that you've never known before?

Are you someone who wants the kind of income that can transform your lifestyle?

If your answer is yes, then I honestly can't wait to work with you!

MY MISSION

I am going to personally help create over 1,000 digital publishers. We are going to completely change the future of the information world.

We are going to create millions and millions of dollars of wealth for our community. I want to invite you into that community. I want to guide you. I want to throw all of my resources behind you.

Moving forward, I will make a few personal recommendations:

1 – www.Lurn.com
Please explore our website to learn more about the programs we offer and how we can personally help you build your business.

2 – Subscribe to our newsletter.
We have an additional free book you can receive by going to www.Lurn.com and simply subscribing to our free newsletter. In this free book, I give you a very guided approach to launching your own information product.

3 – Join our blog community!
This is the first step to becoming a part of our Lurn Nation. Please come by our blog, introduce yourself, and absorb the amazing information we have prepared for you.

4 – Enroll in our courses and training.
The two programs I recommend the most are:

Inbox Blueprint:
Teaches you how to build an email marketing business and provides you with the industry's #1 technology to help you launch your business in less than 60 minutes. www.InboxBlueprint.com

Publish Academy:
Teaches you how to publish your first course online and how to quickly begin producing profits from it. This community is rated the best training and hand-holding coaching you can find when it comes to digital publishing. Please come visit us to learn more at www.PublishAcademy.com.

Welcome to your new successful life.

OTHER RESOURCES FROM THE AUTHOR

BOOKS BY ANIK SINGAL

The Circle of Profit
How To Turn Your Passion Into A Profitable Business
For more information please go to: www.thecircleofprofit.com

The Email Lifeline
How To Increase Your Email Marketing Profits By 300% Using A Simple Formula

LURN ONLINE COURSES

Inbox Blueprint
For more information please visit www.inboxblueprint.com

Publish Academy
For more information please visit www.publishacademy.com

List Academy
For more information please visit www.listacademy.com

OTHER RESOURCES

Please visit our Lurn Blog for updates and free content. www.lurn.com/blog

EARNING DISCLAIMER

The information you'll find in this book is to educate you. We make no promise or guarantee of income or earnings. You have to do some work, use your best judgment, and perform due diligence before using the information in this book. Your success is still up to you.

Nothing in this book is intended to be professional, legal, financial and/or accounting advice. Always seek competent advice from professionals in these matters. We also recommend that you check all local, state, and federal laws to make sure you are in compliance when you create your online business. If you break federal, state, city, or other local laws, we will not be held liable for any damages you incur.

INDEX